LAKE GARDA

TRAVEL GUIDE 2025

Your Ultimate Guide To Exploring Italy's Most Enchanting Lake In 2025

By

PAMELA BEBIR

Copyright © 2025 PAMELA BEBIR. This comprehensive book entitled "Lake Garda: Your Ultimate Guide To Exploring Italy's Most Enchanting Lake 2025" is protected by international copyright laws. All rights, including reproduction, distribution, or transmission of any portion of this guide in any format, require explicit written consent from the author. Unauthorized use or duplication of this travel guide is strictly prohibited and may result in legal action. Your respect for the author's creative work is greatly appreciated.

TABLE OF CONTENT

INTRODUCTION TO LAKE GARDA 8
1.1 Geography: The Regions of Lake Garda 9
1.2 Climate and Natural Environment 11

PLANNING YOUR TRIP TO LAKE GARDA 15
2.1 When to Visit: Seasons and Weather 15
2.2 How to Get There: Airports, Trains and Roads 17
2.3 Navigating the Lake: Ferries, Cars, and Bicycles 20

DISCOVERING LAKE GARDA'S TOWNS 24
3.1 Northern Shore 24
3.2 Western Shore 27
3.3 Eastern Shore 29
3.4 Southern Shore 30

TOP EXPERIENCES AND ATTRACTIONS 32
4.1 Historical Landmarks and Castles 32
4.2 Outdoor Adventures: Hiking, Cycling and Climbing 36
4.3 Water Activities: Sailing, Swimming and Kayaking 38
4.4 Exploring the Olive Oil and Wine Routes of Lake Garda 40

CULTURAL HIGHLIGHTS 44
5.1 Local Traditions and Customs of Lake Garda 44
5.2 Art and Music Festivals of Lake Garda 46
5.3 Entertainment And Nightlife 47
5.4 Historical Museums and Galleries of Lake Garda 48
5.5 Shopping 51

ACCOMMODATION OPTION 54
6.1 Boutique Hotels and Luxury Resorts 54
6.2 Budget friendly Guesthouse 55
6.3 Camping Site for Outdoor Enthusiast 56

WHAT TO EAT AND DRINK 59
7.1 Traditional Dishes of Lake Garda 59
7.2 Local wines: Bardolino and Laguna 60
7.3 Olive Oils 61
7.4 Best Restaurants and Hidden Gems 62

DAY TRIPS AND EXCURSIONS 63

    8.1 Discovering the Dolomite.. 63
    8.2 Verona: The City of Love.. 65
    8.3 Venice: A Romantic Getaway... 67
    8.4 Gardaland and Caneva Aquapark: Family Fun and Adventure . 69
    8.5 Boat Tour And Cruise Lake Garda... 72
ITINERARY.. 75
    9.1 5-Day Itinerary for Lake Garda: Exploring the Best of the Lake 75
PRACTICAL TIPS FOR TRAVELLERS... 79
    10.1 Essential travel documents.. 79
    10.2 Language basics and local phrases... 81
    10.3 Currency for Lake Garda.. 84

Bonuses :

- **Travel planner**
- **The City's general map**

Are you ready to explore the hidden gems of Lake Garda's beauties? If your answer is in affirmative, then come along with me

WHAT TO EXPECT FROM THIS GUIDEBOOK

Welcome to Lake Garda. This comprehensive travel guide is your ultimate companion to discovering the wonders of Lake Garda. Whether you're a seasoned traveler or planning your first trip, this guide is packed with detailed insights, practical tips, and exciting recommendations to ensure you make the most of your journey.

Map Navigation

Navigate Lake Garda like a pro with detailed guidance on how to get around. Lake Garda, Italy's largest lake, is surrounded by picturesque towns and stunning landscapes, this guide provides easy-to-follow tips on map reading and digital tools to help you explore with confidence

Accommodation Options

Lake Garda offers a wide range of accommodations to suit every budget and preference, from luxury resorts to budget-friendly guesthouses. Each option includes pricing, amenities, and ideal locations to suit your preferences and budget.

Transportation

Learn how to move seamlessly around Lake Garda with information on public transportation, car rentals, taxis, and domestic flights. Tips on fares, routes, and safety will help you travel stress-free, whether you're exploring surrounding cities or remote villages.

Top Tourist Attractions

This guide highlights Lake Garda's most iconic landmarks, from historic castles and ancient ruins to vibrant cultural hubs and scenic vistas. Discover must-visit spots, complete with practical details like opening hours, entrance fees, and insider tips for avoiding crowds.

Sightseeing Tours

This guide offers curated recommendations for guided tours, from serene boat cruises and vineyard excursions to adventurous hiking and cycling experiences. You'll find options tailored to various interests, complete with booking details, pricing, and insider tips for making the most of your tour.

Outdoor Activities and Adventure

showcasing, the best ways to immerse yourself in Lake Garda's natural beauty, from exhilarating water sports like sailing and kayaking to serene hiking and cycling trails. Packed with practical tips, safety advice, and recommended spots

Off-the-Beaten-Path Hidden Gems

From secret gardens and quirky markets to lesser-known museums and historic inns, this section reveals Lake Garda's charming and lesser-explored corners.

Shopping

Discover the vibrant world of Lake Garda shopping, from bustling souks to chic boutique stores. Learn about must-buy items such as handcrafted rugs, leather goods, and olive oil. Tips on bargaining and the best shopping districts will ensure you leave with treasures.

Day Trips and Excursions

Plan unforgettable day trips from Lake Garda, including visits to the romantic streets of Verona, the breathtaking Dolomites, and the iconic canals of Venice. Detailed itineraries and transportation tips make these excursions hassle-free.

Entertainment and Nightlife

From lively lakeside bars and chic wine lounges to cultural events and music festivals. Whether you're seeking a quiet evening with local wines or an energetic night at a club, you'll find curated recommendations and insider tips to enjoy the lake after dark.

Practicable Itinerary

Follow a well-crafted 5-day itinerary that takes you through the Lake's Facts, blending culture, adventure, and relaxation for a balanced and memorable trip.

Practical Information and Travel Resources

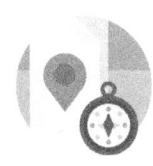

Stay informed with essential travel information, including currency exchange, language tips, safety guidelines, and emergency contacts. You'll also find advice on connectivity, cultural norms, and resources for travelers with special needs.

Culinary Delights

Introducing you to Lake Garda's rich culinary scene, featuring local specialties like olive oils, fresh fish, and regional wines. You'll discover the best restaurants, food markets, and unique dining experiences, along with recommendations for must-try dishes and drinks to make your trip truly flavorful

Culture and Heritage

Lake Garda's rich cultural history, showcasing its art, architecture, and local traditions. Expect detailed insights into historic landmarks, museums, festivals, and the region's unique blend of Italian

CHAPTER 1

INTRODUCTION TO LAKE GARDA

Last summer, I stood on the shores of Lake Garda, Italy's largest and perhaps most captivating lake, and felt as though I had stepped into a dream. The gentle waves lapped at my feet as the sun dipped behind the surrounding mountains, casting a golden glow over the water. A soft breeze carried the scent of olive groves and wildflowers, mingling with the distant laughter of families enjoying an evening stroll. In that moment, I understood why Lake Garda has been a haven for poets, painters, and dreamers for centuries.

Lake Garda isn't just a destination; it's an experience. From the medieval streets of Malcesine crowned by its fairy-tale castle to the vibrant vineyards of Bardolino producing some of Italy's finest wines, every corner of this region tells a story. I remember savoring my first bite of freshly made tortellini in a family-run trattoria in Sirmione, where the owners treated me more like family than a visitor. The warmth of their hospitality was as unforgettable as the breathtaking view of the lake from their terrace.

8

One morning, I hiked through the trails above Riva del Garda, rewarded by panoramic views that made the climb worthwhile. Later, I took a ferry to Limone sul Garda, a charming village perched precariously on the cliffs, where lemon trees thrive in the Mediterranean sunshine. Each day brought new adventures—cycling along the waterfront, exploring ancient Roman ruins, or simply losing myself in the beauty of the landscape.

What makes Lake Garda truly magical is its ability to appeal to every traveler. Whether you seek romance, adventure, culture, or tranquility, the lake offers it all in abundance. As I write this, I still hear the soft melodies of the street musicians in Desenzano and feel the cool waters from a midday swim.

Lake Garda stole my heart that summer, and I promise it will steal yours too. Let me guide you through this enchanting corner of Italy, so you can create your own unforgettable memories.

1.1 Geography: The Regions of Lake Garda

Lake Garda, Italy's largest lake, spans approximately 370 square kilometers (143 square miles) and is nestled at the intersection of three regions: Lombardy to the west, Veneto to the east, and Trentino-Alto Adige to the north. This unique positioning endows the lake with a diverse blend of landscapes, climates, and cultural influences, making it a captivating destination for travelers.

Northern Shore: Trentino-Alto Adige: The northern extremity of Lake Garda is characterized by its fjord-like appearance, with steep mountains such as Monte Baldo and the Alpi Ledrensi enclosing the lake. This area is renowned for its alpine scenery, making it a haven for outdoor enthusiasts.

Riva del Garda: A vibrant town known for its medieval architecture and as a hub for sailing and windsurfing.

Torbole: A picturesque village favored by windsurfers due to its consistent winds.

Outdoor Activities: The consistent winds in this area make it ideal for windsurfing and sailing.

Cultural Blend: The region exhibits a unique mix of Italian and Germanic influences, evident in its architecture and local traditions.

Western Shore: Lombardy: The western shore, part of the Lombardy region, is distinguished by its lush vegetation, including evergreen plants and trees. This area offers a serene environment with charming towns and historical sites.

Limone sul Garda: Famous for its terraced lemon groves and narrow, winding streets.

Gargnano: A tranquil village known for its historic villas and serene atmosphere.

Salò: A town with a rich history and a beautiful lakeside promenade.

Mediterranean Climate: The mild climate supports a variety of Mediterranean vegetation, including olive trees and lemon groves.

Scenic Drives: The western shore offers picturesque routes with stunning lake views.

Eastern Shore: Located in Veneto. The eastern shore falls within the Veneto region and is rich in Mediterranean vegetation. This area is known for its charming towns, vineyards, and historical sites.

Malcesine: Dominated by the Scaliger Castle, it offers medieval charm and access to Monte Baldo via cable car.

Bardolino: Renowned for its wine production, particularly the Bardolino red wine.

Lazise: A town with medieval walls and a picturesque harbor.

Wine Production: The region is famous for its vineyards and wine festivals.

Monte Baldo: Accessible via cable car from Malcesine, offering panoramic views and hiking opportunities.

Southern Shore: The southern shore of Lake Garda is characterized by a mix of cultural influences and a diverse landscape.

Desenzano del Garda: A bustling town with a vibrant nightlife and historical sites.
Sirmione: Located on a peninsula, it is known for its thermal baths and the Grottoes of Catullus.
Thermal Springs: Sirmione is famous for its thermal waters and wellness centers.

Historical Sites: The southern shore boasts Roman ruins and medieval castles.

- **Islands of Lake Garda**: Lake Garda is home to several islands, each with its own unique charm.

- **Isola del Garda:** The largest island, known for its Venetian-style villa and lush gardens.

- **Isola di San Biagio** (Isola dei Conigli): Also known as the "Island of the Rabbits," it is a popular spot for swimming and picnics. Isola dell'Olivo, Isola di Sogno, and Isola di Trimelone: Smaller islands that add to the lake's scenic beauty.

1.2 Climate and Natural Environment

The lake's particularly mild climate favors the growth of Mediterranean plants, including olive trees, parasol pines, cypresses, and certain citrus trees. This unique microclimate has made Lake Garda a popular destination for visitors seeking both relaxation and outdoor activities. Lake Garda's diverse geography, spanning three regions, offers a rich tapestry of landscapes and cultural experiences. From the alpine terrains of the north to the rolling vineyards of the east and the historical towns of the south, each area provides unique attractions that cater to a wide range of interests. Lake Garda, Italy's largest lake, boasts a rich and varied history that mirrors the broader historical currents of the region. From its geological formation to its role in modern tourism, the lake has been a focal point for human activity and settlement.

Geological Formation

Lake Garda was formed during the Quaternary Ice Ages by a massive glacier, which sculpted its current shape and contributed to the fertility of the surrounding soil.

Prehistoric Inhabitants

Archaeological findings indicate human presence around Lake Garda dating back to the Middle Paleolithic era, with flint tools discovered at higher altitudes. Evidence of Upper Paleolithic encampments has been found on the slopes of Monte Baldo and Stivo.

Roman Era

During Roman times, the lake was known as Lacus Benacus and was mentioned by classical writers such as Virgil, Horace, and Catullus. The area became an integral part of the Roman Empire, serving as a key route for trade and military operations. Wealthy Romans constructed luxurious villas along the shores, with notable remnants like the Grottoes of Catullus in Sirmione still standing today.

Medieval Period

In the early 9th century, the city of Garda was elevated to a county by Emperor Charlemagne, leading to the lake's name change from Lacus Benacus to Lake Garda. During the medieval era, the region saw the construction of numerous castles and fortifications, many of which remain as historical monuments today.

Venetian and Austrian Influence

The Republic of Venice extended its influence over parts of Lake Garda, particularly the eastern shore, fostering trade and cultural development. Following the fall of Venice in 1797, the Treaty of Campo Formio ceded Lake Garda to Austria. The northern end of the lake remained under Austrian control until 1919.

Modern Era

In the 20th century, Lake Garda became a significant tourist destination, renowned for its natural beauty and historical significance. The construction of the Gardesana scenic route, completed in 1931, enhanced accessibility and tourism around the lake.

Recent Developments

Today, Lake Garda continues to attract visitors worldwide, offering a blend of historical sites, cultural experiences, and recreational activities. The region has seen efforts to preserve its rich history while accommodating modern tourism, ensuring that the legacy of Lake Garda endures for future generations.

Lake Garda's history is a testament to its enduring appeal and significance, from its geological origins to its current status as a premier tourist destination.

CHAPTER 2

PLANNING YOUR TRIP TO LAKE GARDA

2.1 When to Visit: Seasons and Weather

Planning a trip to Lake Garda involves careful consideration of the timing, as the region's climate varies significantly throughout the year. Here's an extensive guide to help you choose the best time to visit, based on seasonal weather patterns and activities.

Spring (March to May)

Spring is a delightful time to visit Lake Garda, with temperatures gradually rising from around 10°C (50°F) in March to 20°C (68°F) in May. The landscape comes alive with blooming flowers, making it ideal for outdoor activities like hiking and cycling. However, be prepared for occasional rain showers during this period.

Summer (June to August)

Summer is the peak tourist season at Lake Garda, characterized by warm temperatures averaging between 25°C (77°F) and 30°C

(86°F). July is typically the hottest month, with average highs of 28°C (82°F). This season is perfect for water sports, beach relaxation, and enjoying the vibrant atmosphere of lakeside towns. Keep in mind that this is also the busiest time, so expect larger crowds and higher accommodation prices.

Autumn (September to November)
Autumn offers a more tranquil experience, with temperatures ranging from 20°C (68°F) in September to 10°C (50°F) in November. September is particularly pleasant, often referred to as the "second summer," providing warm weather without the summer crowds. This period is excellent for wine tours, as the grape harvest occurs, and for exploring cultural sites. Note that rainfall can increase in autumn, especially in September, which is the wettest month with an average of 86mm of rain.

Winter (December to February)
Winter is the off-season at Lake Garda, with temperatures dropping to an average low of 2°C (36°F) in January, the coldest month. While some attractions may have limited hours, this season offers a peaceful retreat with fewer tourists. It's an ideal time for those interested in spa experiences, local cuisine, and exploring the charming, quiet streets of lakeside villages.

Recommendations

Best Time to Visit: For pleasant weather and manageable crowds, consider visiting in late spring (mid-April to mid-June) or early autumn (September). These periods offer comfortable temperatures and beautiful natural scenery.
Peak Season: If you prefer a lively atmosphere with numerous events and activities, summer is the ideal time, keeping in mind the higher tourist density.
Off-Season: For a serene experience and lower prices, winter provides a unique charm, though some facilities may have reduced availability.

When planning your trip, consider the types of activities you wish to engage in and choose the season that best aligns with your preferences. Always check the latest weather forecasts and local event calendars to make the most of your visit to Lake Garda.

2.2 How to Get There: Airports, Trains and Roads

Lake Garda is easily accessible from various parts of Europe and beyond, thanks to its well-connected transportation network. Here's an extensive guide to getting to this breathtaking destination, whether you're flying, taking the train, or driving.

By Air: Airports Near Lake Garda

Lake Garda is served by several international and regional airports, making it convenient for travelers flying in from different locations.

Verona Villafranca Airport (VRN)

Distance: About 15 km (9 miles) from the southern shores of Lake Garda.
Best For: Travelers heading to towns like Peschiera del Garda, Lazise, and Bardolino.
Transport Options: Shuttle buses to Verona city center and onward trains to Lake Garda towns. Car rentals and taxis available at the airport.

Bergamo Orio al Serio Airport (BGY)

Distance: Approximately 80 km (50 miles) from the lake.
Best For: Budget airlines like Ryanair and towns on the western side of the lake.
Transport Options:
Buses to Brescia or Milan, with train connections to Lake Garda.

Milan Airports
Milan Malpensa Airport (MXP): 160 km (100 miles) from the lake.
Milan Linate Airport (LIN): 130 km (81 miles) from the lake.

Best For: International travelers with options for both eastern and western shores.

Venice Marco Polo Airport (VCE)
Distance: About 150 km (93 miles) from the lake.
Best For: Visitors combining Lake Garda with Venice.
Transport Options: Train and bus connections via Venice Mestre or Verona.
Bologna Guglielmo Marconi Airport (BLQ) – 140 km (87 miles).
Innsbruck Airport (INN), Austria – Ideal for northern visitors, 210 km (130 miles).

By Train: Rail Connections to Lake Garda

Lake Garda's proximity to major Italian cities makes it accessible via a well-established train network.

Main Train Stations Around Lake Garda

Desenzano del Garda-Sirmione: Serves the southern shore; connected by high-speed trains.
Peschiera del Garda: Another major station on the southern shore, close to Gardaland theme park.
Rovereto: Closest station for the northern towns, such as Riva del Garda.

Key Train Routes

From Milan: Trains to Desenzano or Peschiera del Garda take about 1–1.5 hours.
From Venice: Regular trains to Desenzano or Peschiera take around 1.5–2 hours.
From Verona: Frequent regional trains to Desenzano or Peschiera, taking 20–30 minutes.

Tips: Book tickets in advance for high-speed trains (Frecciarossa or Italo) for better prices. Regional trains are more affordable and do not require reservations.

By Road: Driving to Lake Garda

Driving offers the most flexibility to explore Lake Garda and its charming towns.

Key Highways: A4 Autostrada (Milan-Venice): Runs along the southern shore of the lake.
A22 Autostrada del Brennero (Modena-Brenner): Best for accessing the northern shore.

Main Exits
Peschiera del Garda (A4): Southern access to towns like Lazise and Bardolino.
Desenzano del Garda (A4): Gateway to the western shore.
Rovereto Sud/Lago di Garda Nord (A22): Ideal for northern towns like Riva del Garda.

Driving Times
From Milan: ~2 hours (140 km/87 miles).
From Venice: ~2 hours (150 km/93 miles).
From Bologna: ~2.5 hours (170 km/106 miles).

Car Rental and Parking
Car rentals are available at airports and major cities.
Parking is plentiful but can be limited in popular towns during peak seasons.

Visit: www.carflexi.com for rental booking

By Bus: Local and Long-Distance Options
Long-Distance Buses
FlixBus and similar services connect Lake Garda to cities like Milan, Venice, and Florence.

Drop-off points are usually in Desenzano or Peschiera del Garda.
Local Buses. Operated by ATV and other regional companies.
Connects smaller towns like Garda, Malcesine, and Riva del Garda.

2.3 Navigating the Lake: Ferries, Cars, and Bicycles

Navigating Lake Garda offers a variety of transportation options, each providing a unique experience of this stunning region. Whether you prefer the scenic routes of ferries, the flexibility of driving, or the eco-friendly choice of cycling, here's an extensive guide to help you plan your journey.

Ferries: Scenic and Efficient. Lake Garda's ferry system is an excellent way to explore its picturesque towns and enjoy panoramic views of the lake. Ferry Routes and Timetables: The ferry network connects major towns such as Desenzano del Garda, Sirmione, Peschiera del Garda, Riva del Garda, and Malcesine. Timetables vary seasonally, with more frequent services during the summer months.

Ferry Fares: Ticket prices depend on the route and type of service (e.g., standard ferry, hydrofoil). As of the latest available information, single journey fares start from approximately €3 (about

$3.30 USD). For example, a one-way ticket from Desenzano del Garda to Sirmione costs around €3. For longer routes, such as from Desenzano del Garda to Riva del Garda, fares can be higher.

Car Rentals: Flexibility and Convenience. Renting a car provides the freedom to explore Lake Garda and its surroundings at your own pace.

Rental Locations: Car rental services are available in major towns around the lake, including Desenzano del Garda, Peschiera del Garda, and Riva del Garda. International rental companies such as Avis, Europcar, and Hertz operate in the area.

Rental Prices: Rental rates vary based on the vehicle type, rental duration, and season. On average, expect to pay around $56 per day. For a week-long rental, prices can range from $307 to $350, depending on the car model and rental company. It's advisable to book in advance, especially during peak tourist seasons, to secure the best rates.

Bicycle Rentals: Eco-Friendly Exploration. Cycling around Lake Garda is a popular activity, offering both locals and tourists a chance to enjoy the natural beauty and charming villages.

Rental Services: Several rental shops around the lake offer a variety of bicycles, including city bikes, mountain bikes, and electric bikes. Notable providers include Velolake, which has locations in Torbole, Peschiera del Garda, and Bardolino, and CCT Bike Rental, offering delivery services to various locations.

Rental Prices: Rental rates depend on the bike type and rental duration. For instance, a city bike may cost around €31 (approximately $34 USD) for two days, while an electric mountain bike can be rented for about €82 (around $90 USD) for two days. Electric bikes are particularly popular for navigating the lake's varied terrain.

Rental Service to Book:

For car rentals at Lake Garda, a reliable option for booking is Kayak, which provides a range of rental services from multiple agencies at competitive prices. Here's how you can easily book a car rental:

Car Rental Booking Service:

Kayak: Book a Car Rental on Kayak. Kayak compares prices from various car rental companies, ensuring you find the best deals for your travel dates. Available pickup locations include towns around Lake Garda such as Desenzano del Garda, Peschiera del Garda, and Riva del Garda. Prices typically start at $56 per day, and you can reserve your rental in advance to lock in the best rates. Booking through Kayak ensures flexibility and a wide selection of vehicles, from compact cars to larger SUVs, allowing you to explore the beautiful lake region comfortably.

Ferry Booking Service:

Navigazione Laghi: Book Ferries on Navigazione Laghi. This is the official ferry service for Lake Garda, connecting major towns such as Desenzano del Garda, Sirmione, Peschiera del Garda, and Riva del GardaFor instance, a one-way ticket starts at approximately $3.30 USD (around €3) depending on the route. During the peak season, it's recommended to book tickets in advance to secure your spot.

Bicycle Rental Services:

Velolake: Book Bikes on Velolake. Velolake offers bicycle rentals at multiple locations around Lake Garda, including Peschiera del Garda, Bardolino, and Torbole.You can rent city bikes, mountain bikes, and e-bikes, with delivery options available to your hotel.Prices for city bikes start at approximately $17 per day, while electric bikes start from around $45 per day.

CCT Bike Rental: Book Bikes on CCT Bike Rental

CCT Bike Rental offers a variety of bikes for different terrains, including electric bikes, mountain bikes, and road bikes. They provide delivery services, which means the bikes can be dropped off directly at your hotel or chosen location.Rental prices for electric bikes start around $50 USD per day.

CHAPTER 3

DISCOVERING LAKE GARDA'S TOWNS

The towns surrounding Lake Garda each offer a unique charm, from historical landmarks to outdoor adventures. The northern shore, with its dramatic cliffs and serene atmosphere, is particularly captivating.

3.1 Northern Shore

Riva del Garda: Nestled at the northern tip of Lake Garda, Riva del

Garda is one of the most picturesque towns on the lake. It is surrounded by towering mountains and lush landscapes, making it a perfect spot for nature lovers and adventure enthusiasts.

Outdoor Activities:Riva del Garda is known for its abundance of outdoor activities. The town is a mecca for hikers, mountain bikers, and climbers, with trails offering panoramic views of the lake and the surrounding mountains. The nearby Monte Baldo is a popular hiking and biking destination, accessible by cable car or on foot.

Cycling: The town has many cycling routes that attract tourists and professional cyclists alike. The Garda by Bike program provides well-marked paths for cyclists, offering a blend of scenic views and challenging terrain.

Climbing and Paragliding: The mountains around Riva del Garda offer some of the best climbing routes in Italy, and the town's location near the wind corridor makes it a top spot for paragliding.

Historical Sites:
Riva del Garda also boasts historical charm. Piazza III Novembre is the heart of the town, surrounded by stunning buildings such as the Torre Apponale, a medieval tower offering fantastic views of the town and lake. The Museo Alto Garda showcases local history and art, including the fascinating archaeological findings from the area.

Lake Activities:
The lake itself is perfect for water sports, including kayaking, sailing, and windsurfing. Riva del Garda's Porto San Nicolò is a hub for boating activities, with plenty of boat rentals and excursions available.

Torbole: Windsurfing Capital
Just a short distance from Riva del Garda, the town of Torbole is a magnet for water sports enthusiasts, particularly windsurfers. Situated on the northeastern shore of Lake Garda, it is known as the windsurfing capital of the lake, thanks to the perfect wind conditions that are ideal for this sport.

Windsurfing and Sailing:
Torbole's consistent winds, particularly the Ora (a thermal breeze that picks up in the afternoon), create ideal conditions for windsurfing, kite surfing, and sailing. The beach area in Porto di

Torbole is lined with schools and rental shops for those wishing to learn or rent equipment.

Windsurfing Events: Torbole hosts various international windsurfing competitions, making it a prime destination for professionals and enthusiasts. One of the most famous events is the Wind Festival, which celebrates the town's rich history in windsurfing.

Beaches and Relaxation: Although Torbole is famous for its adventure sports, it also offers peaceful lakeside relaxation. The Lido di Torbole is a popular spot for swimming and sunbathing, with crystal-clear water and stunning views of the surrounding mountains.

Cycling and Hiking:

Similar to Riva del Garda, Torbole is surrounded by beautiful landscapes, ideal for cycling and hiking. The Busatte-Tempesta Trail is a must-do for hiking enthusiasts, offering panoramic views of the lake and a challenge for seasoned hikers.

Charming Streets and Local Cuisine:

The town itself has a lovely, small-town charm with its cobblestone streets and charming cafes. Visitors can indulge in traditional Italian cuisine, including fresh fish from the lake, as well as regional specialties such as polenta and torta delle rose (rose-shaped cake).

Best Time to Visit

The best time to visit these northern towns is during the late spring and summer months (May to September). The weather is perfect for outdoor activities, and the winds for windsurfing are most reliable during this time. If you prefer a quieter visit, consider coming in early spring or fall when the crowds are fewer, and the natural scenery is still magnificent.

3.2 Western Shore

The western shore of Lake Garda is renowned for its dramatic landscapes, charming towns, and rich history. From the fragrant lemon groves of Limone sul Garda to the tranquil retreats of Gargnano and Salò, and the historic allure of Sirmione, this region offers a diverse array of experiences.

Limone sul Garda:Limone sul Garda, often referred to as the "Lemon Town," is celebrated for its centuries-old lemon cultivation traditions. The town's terraced lemon groves, known as "limoneti," are a testament to its agricultural heritage. Visitors can explore the Limonaia del Castèl, a historical lemon garden that offers insights into the town's citrus-growing past. The town's narrow streets are lined with charming shops, cafes, and restaurants, many of which overlook the lake. The historical Piazza San Giovanni is home to the town's church and is an ideal spot to relax and enjoy a coffee.

Gargnano: Gargnano is one of the quieter towns on Lake Garda, making it perfect for those seeking a relaxing escape. The town is set against the backdrop of steep mountains and lush olive groves, providing a tranquil and picturesque setting. For those who enjoy outdoor activities, Gargnano offers a variety of walking and cycling trails through olive groves and forests. There are also several boat tours available from the town, giving visitors a chance to explore the lake's hidden coves.

Salò: Salò is one of Lake Garda's more sophisticated towns, known for its elegant lakeside promenade lined with cafes, boutiques, and restaurants. The town boasts a stunning view of the lake and the surrounding mountains, with plenty of spots to relax and enjoy the view. The town is rich in history, with landmarks such as the Cathedral of Santa Maria Annunziata, a beautiful church with a striking bell tower, and the Palazzo della Magnifica Patria, a historic building that houses local government offices and a museum. Salò offers easy access to the lake for those interested in water activities, including sailing, kayaking, and swimming. The nearby Parco Alto Garda Bresciano provides additional hiking and nature trails for outdoor enthusiasts.

Sirmione: Sirmione is often referred to as the *"Pearl of Lake Garda,"* and it's easy to see why. This enchanting town sits on a narrow peninsula that juts out into the southern part of the lake, offering unparalleled views and a rich history. One of Sirmione's most famous landmarks is the Scaliger Castle, a 13th-century fortress that stands proudly at the entrance to the town. The castle is well-preserved and offers stunning views of the lake and surrounding areas from its towers. Visitors can explore the castle's ramparts, courtyards, and museum. Sirmione is also known for its thermal waters, which have been used for therapeutic purposes since Roman times. The

Terme di Sirmione spa complex offers visitors a chance to relax and unwind in the healing waters, making it a popular destination for wellness tourism.

3.3 Eastern Shore

The eastern shore of Lake Garda is celebrated for its enchanting towns, each offering unique experiences. Here's an overview of Malcesine, Bardolino, and Lazise, highlighting their distinctive features.

Malcesine: Malcesine is renowned for its medieval charm, dominated by the impressive Scaliger Castle overlooking Lake Garda. The town's narrow cobblestone streets, lined with quaint shops and cafes, lead to the lakeshore, offering stunning views and a relaxed atmosphere.

Recently, Malcesine has been a hub for cultural events. The Malcesine Music Festival is scheduled for July 12 to September 6, featuring concerts at the Pacengo harbour every evening at 9 PM.

Bardolino and Lazise: Wine Lover's Paradise

Bardolino and Lazise are picturesque towns known for their vineyards, olive groves, and charming lakeside promenades.

Bardolino: This town is renowned for its vineyards that produce the famous Bardolino DOC wines. Wine enthusiasts can explore the surrounding vineyards, visit local wineries, and indulge in wine tasting experiences. Bardolino's annual wine festivals also attract crowds from all over the world, offering a great way to experience the region's wine culture.

Lazise: Just a short distance from Bardolino, Lazise is a delightful medieval town with a rich history. Its charming old town is filled with narrow streets, while the stunning Lazise Castle stands as a testament to the town's past. Lazise is also home to Gardaland, one of Italy's largest theme parks, making it a popular destination for families.

3.4 Southern Shore

The southern shore of Lake Garda is home to two of its most vibrant towns: Desenzano del Garda and Peschiera del Garda. Each offers a unique blend of history, culture, and modern amenities.

Desenzano del Garda: Desenzano del Garda is the largest town on the southern shore, known for its lively atmosphere and rich history. The town boasts a bustling port, a vibrant town center, and a variety of shops, cafes, and restaurants.

Recent Developments: Transportation Updates: As of January 10, 2025, the Peschiera del Garda toll booth will be closed for approximately 24 days due to construction work related to the new high-speed railway line. This may affect traffic flow in the area.

Cultural Events: Desenzano continues to host various cultural events and festivals throughout the year, attracting both locals and tourists. For the latest information on upcoming events, visitors are encouraged to check local event calendars.

Peschiera del Garda: Peschiera del Garda is a UNESCO World Heritage site, celebrated for its well-preserved Renaissance-era fortifications and its strategic location at the mouth of the Mincio River. The town features charming canals, historic buildings, and a relaxed lakeside ambiance.

Recent Developments:Traffic Incidents: Recently, there have been reports of traffic incidents on the A4 motorway between Sirmione and Peschiera, leading to delays and congestion. Travelers are advised to check traffic updates before planning their journeys.

Community Events: Peschiera del Garda hosts various community events, including local festivals and markets. For instance, the town celebrated the feast of its patron saint, San Martino, with gastronomic stands and fireworks.

CHAPTER 4

TOP EXPERIENCES AND ATTRACTIONS

4.1 Historical Landmarks and Castles

Lake Garda, Italy's largest lake, is adorned with numerous historical landmarks and castles that offer a glimpse into its rich past. Here are some of the most notable ones:

Scaliger Castle (Castello Scaligero): Located in the town of Sirmione, this 13th-century fortress is one of Italy's best-preserved castles. It features a moat, drawbridge, and towers, providing panoramic views of Lake Garda. The castle houses a museum showcasing artifacts from the region's history.

Opening Hours: Summer (April 1st - September 30th):

Tuesday to Saturday: 8:30 AM – 7:30 PM (last entry at 6:45 PM)
Sunday and holidays: 9:15 AM – 5:45 PM (last entry at 5:00 PM)

Winter (October 1st - March 31st):

Tuesday to Saturday: 8:30 AM – 7:30 PM (last entry at 6:45 PM)
Sunday: 8:30 AM – 1:30 PM (last entry at 12:45 PM)
Holidays: 8:30 AM – 7:30 PM (last entry at 6:45 PM)

Entrance Fees: Full price: €8 ($9); EU citizens (18-25 years old): €3 ($4); Children (up to 18): Free

Scaliger Castle: Situated in Malcesine, this medieval castle offers stunning views of the lake and surrounding mountains. It now hosts the Natural History Museum of Garda and Monte Baldo, providing insights into the area's natural heritage.

Opening Hours: March 11th to November 3rd:
Daily: 9:30 AM – 6:30 PM

Entrance Fees: Adults: €6.00 ($6); Students and over 65: €5.00($5); Children (6-18 years): €3.00 ($3); Children (0-6 years): Free

Rocca di Riva: Located in Riva del Garda. This medieval fortress, located on a small artificial island, was built in 1124 to defend the port of Riva del Garda. It now serves as a museum, offering exhibitions on local history and art. Opens from 10 a.m. to 6 p.m., but the days of operation vary depending on the time of year. From March 16 to May 31 and from October 1 to November 3, it's open Tuesday to Sunday. During the peak season, from June 1 to September 30, it's open every day. There are also special opening periods from November 30 to December 15 and from December 20 to January 6. As for the entrance fee, it costs €5 to get in. However, if you have the Trentino Card, you can enter for free.

Grotte di Catullo: Located in Sirmione. These ancient Roman ruins are the remnants of a grand villa believed to have been built in the 1st century AD. Visitors can explore the archaeological site and enjoy panoramic views of the lake. The Grotte di Catullo in Sirmione is open from Tuesday to Sunday, with varying hours depending on the time of year. During the summer months, from the last Sunday in March to the last Saturday in October, the site is open from 8:30 AM to 7:30 PM. In the winter, it's open from 8:30 AM to 5:00 PM, with the ticket office closing 50 minutes before the site closes.

As for the entrance fee, a standard ticket costs €8, while a reduced ticket for EU citizens between 18 and 25 years old costs €2. Admission is free for people under 18 years old, students, and school teachers. It's worth noting that you can also purchase a cumulative ticket that grants access to the Scaligero Castle in Sirmione, the Grottoes of Catullus archaeological site, and the Archaeological Museum and Villa Romana di Desenzano. This ticket costs €14 for a full ticket and €6 for a reduced ticket.

Vittoriale degli Italiani : Located Gardone Riviera. This monumental complex was the residence of poet Gabriele D'Annunzio. It includes a villa, museum, and amphitheater, reflecting the eclectic tastes of its former owner.

Opening hours Closed on 24 and 25 December, on New Year's Day and from 13 to 17 January 2025.
Closed every Monday and Tuesday in November, December and January (except 30 and 31 December) and every Monday in February.

Entrance Fee: Single ticket: Range from €10.00 - €13.00; Adult groups: €14.00- €20
Student groups: €13.00 - 15

Rocca di Manerba : Located in Manerba del Garda. This fortress offers panoramic views of the lake and is surrounded by a natural park. It's an excellent spot for hiking and exploring the area's flora and fauna.

Open hours
Monday - Sunday
10:00 AM - 6:00 PM

Entrance Fee Adults: €9.00 ($6); Students and over 65: €5.00($5); Children (6-18 years): €3.00 ($3); Children (0-6 years): Free

Castle of Padenghe: Located in Padenghe sul Garda. Overlooking the lake, this castle dates back to the 10th century. While parts of it are in ruins, it remains a significant historical site and offers picturesque views.

Opening time: Tuesday- Saturday 10:00 am - 6:00pm
No entrance fee

Castle of Torri del Benaco: Located in Torri del Benaco. This castle houses the Museum of Lake Garda, providing insights into the region's history and culture. Its towers offer panoramic views of the lake and surrounding areas. Exploring these historical landmarks and castles offers a deep dive into the rich tapestry of Lake Garda's past, each site providing unique insights and breathtaking views.

Opening Time
Spring and Autumn: From April 1 to June 15 and from September 16 to October 31, the castle is open from 9:30 am to 12:30 pm and from 2:30 pm to 6 pm. Summer: From June 16 to September 15, the castle is open from 9:30 am to 1 pm and from 4 pm to 7:30 pm. Winter: The castle's winter hours are from 9:30 am to 12:30 pm and from 2:30 pm to 6 pm, but please note that the castle is closed on Mondays.

Entrance fee: it's quite reasonable:

Adults: €5; Reduced ticket (seniors over 60, groups): €3; Children up to 14 years old: €1; Children under 6 years old and residents: Free admission

4.2 Outdoor Adventures: Hiking, Cycling and Climbing at Lake Garda

Lake Garda is an adventurer's paradise, offering a variety of outdoor activities that cater to thrill-seekers and nature lovers alike. From serene hiking trails to challenging climbing routes and scenic cycling paths, the lake's diverse terrain ensures there's something for everyone.

Hiking: Lake Garda is surrounded by hiking trails that range from gentle walks to challenging mountain treks. These trails offer breathtaking views of the lake, charming villages, and the surrounding Alps.

Popular Trails: Sentiero del Ponale (Ponale Trail); Monte Baldo Summit Trails; Busatte-Tempesta Trail.

Locations: Between Riva del Garda and Valle di Ledro, Monte Baldo Mountain, Near Torbole.

Highlights: Stunning views of the northern shore and Ledro Valley, Panoramic views of Lake Garda and the Dolomites, Dramatic cliffside paths, metal staircases, and lake vistas.

Distance: Approx. 4.5 - 10 km (one-way and round trip)

Difficulty: Easy, moderate to difficult.

Cycling: Pedal Through Paradise

Cycling enthusiasts will find Lake Garda a haven with its dedicated bike paths and off-road mountain biking trails. The lake's perimeter offers flat, family-friendly routes, while the hills challenge experienced riders.

Top Cycling Route:

Garda By Bike:

- Location: Scenic route circling Lake Garda (under construction in parts).
- Difficulty: Easy to moderate
- Highlights: Lakefront views, accessible to all levels.

Rental Services:

- Bike Garda Rental (bike-garda.com): Offers mountain, road, and electric bikes. Rentals start at $20/day.
- Velolake Bike Rental (velolake.com): Specializes in guided tours and premium bike rentals.

Climbing: The northern region of Lake Garda, particularly around Arco, is renowned as a rock climbing mecca. With routes for all skill levels, climbers from around the globe flock here to tackle its limestone cliffs.

Climbing Spots: Colodri Cliff, Massone Climbing Area, Nago Crags

Location: Near Arco, and above Torbole

Difficulty: Easy, moderate to expert

Highlights: Ideal for beginners with well-marked routes, over 100 climbing routes, suitable for advanced climbers and anoramic views of the lake.

Gear Rentals and Guides:

- Vertical Climbing Guides (verticalgarda.com): Provides guided climbs and gear rentals starting at $50/person.

- Arco Climbing Gear Shop (arco-climbing.com): Rent or purchase climbing equipment; guided experiences available.

Planning Tips:

- Best Time for Outdoor Adventures:

Spring (April-May): Pleasant weather, blooming landscapes.

Autumn (September-October): Mild temperatures, fewer crowds.

- Safety: Carry adequate water, sunscreen, and appropriate gear. Check local weather conditions and trail/cliff updates before heading out.

4.3 Water Activities: Sailing, Swimming and Kayaking at Lake Garda

Lake Garda's crystal-clear waters, stunning backdrop, and diverse opportunities make it a hotspot for water activities. Whether you want to glide across the lake on a sailboat, cool off with a swim, or paddle through hidden coves in a kayak, the lake provides unforgettable aquatic adventures.

Sailing: Lake Garda is famous for its consistent winds, making it a dream destination for sailing enthusiasts. The northern part of the lake, particularly around Riva del Garda and Torbole, is ideal due to its stronger winds like the Ora (afternoon breeze) and the Peler (morning wind).

Popular Sailing Spots:

Torbole: Known for its strong winds, perfect for experienced sailors.

Desenzano del Garda: Offers calmer waters for beginners.

Malcesine: Great for both leisure sailing and competitive regattas.

Sailing Schools and Rentals:

- Fraglia Vela Riva (fragliavelariva.com): Provides sailing lessons and rentals, starting at $50/hour.
- Torbole Sailing Club (circolovelatorbole.com): Offers lessons for all skill levels and regatta events.

Swimming: Lake Garda's clean, refreshing waters and numerous beaches provide perfect spots for a swim. Many of the lake's beaches are pebbly, so water shoes are recommended.

Top Swimming Beaches:

- Jamaica Beach (Sirmione): A natural rocky beach with turquoise waters, perfect for sunbathing and swimming.
- Lido di Torbole: Family-friendly with facilities and shallow waters.
- Baia delle Sirene (Garda): A scenic beach with clear water and shaded picnic areas.

Tips for Swimmers:

- Swimming is best from late May to early September when the water temperature averages 22-25°C (72-77°F).
- Most beaches have free entry, but some private beaches charge $5-$15 for access and amenities.

Kayaking: Kayaking on Lake Garda offers a serene way to explore hidden coves, dramatic cliffs, and historic sites like lakeside castles. The calm southern waters are suitable for beginners, while the northern area challenges experienced paddlers.

Top Kayaking Routes:

- Sirmione Peninsula: Paddle around the Scaliger Castle and Grotte di Catullo.
- Limone sul Garda to Tremosine: Explore caves and cliffs along the western shore.

- Isola del Garda: A guided tour to the lake's largest island, with its stunning villa and gardens.

Kayak Rentals and Tours:

- Canoa Kayak Garda (canoakayakgarda.com): Rentals starting at $15/hour and guided tours at $50/person.
- Kayak Garda Adventure (kayakgardaadventure.com): Offers eco-friendly guided experiences and day rentals.

Planning Your Water Adventure

Best Time for Water Activities: Spring (April-June): Mild temperatures and fewer crowds. Summer (July-August): Peak season with warm waters and lively beaches.

Safety Tips: Always wear a life jacket while kayaking or sailing.

Check the weather forecast; sudden storms are rare but possible.

Bring sunscreen, water, and a waterproof bag for essentials.

4.4 Exploring the Olive Oil and Wine Routes of Lake Garda

Lake Garda is not just a visual and adventurous paradise; it's a culinary haven celebrated for its exceptional olive oil and world-class wines. The unique microclimate, shaped by the lake's moderating influence, creates the perfect conditions for olive groves and vineyards to flourish. Embarking on the olive oil and wine routes is an enriching experience that blends history, flavor, and stunning landscapes.

The Olive Oil Route: Lake Garda is one of the northernmost regions in Europe where olive trees thrive, thanks to its Mediterranean-like climate. The Garda DOP (Denominazione di Origine Protetta) olive oil is renowned for its light, fruity flavor and low acidity.

Malcesine Olive Oil Museum:

- Location: Malcesine (eastern shore).
- Highlights: Learn about the traditional oil-making process and sample fresh olive oil.
- Opening Hours: 10 AM - 6 PM.
- Entrance Fee: $5 per person.

Frantoio di Manestrini (Soiano del Lago):

- Location: Western shore near Salò.
- Highlights: Family-owned mill offering guided tours, tastings, and a shop for gourmet products.
- Tours: Starting at $20 per person.

Cisano Olive Oil Museum:

- Location: Bardolino (eastern shore).
- Highlights: Explore ancient tools and methods used in olive oil production.
- Opening Hours: 9 AM - 7 PM.

- Entrance Fee: $6 per person.

Olive Oil Pairing Experiences:

- Many farms offer tastings paired with local bread, cheese, and honey. Reservations are recommended, especially during peak season.

The Wine Route: Lake Garda is home to several prestigious wine regions, each offering its unique grape varieties and styles. The wine route is a sensory journey where you can savor everything from crisp whites to robust reds.

Valtenesi Wine Region (Western Shore): Known for Chiaretto rosé and reds from Groppello grapes.

Must-Try Wine: Valtènesi Chiaretto.

Top Wineries: Azienda Agricola Pasini San Giovanni: A family-run winery with scenic tours.

Wine Tasting Tours and Events:

- Many wineries provide guided tastings, vineyard walks, and pairing experiences with local cuisine.
- Visit during the annual Bardolino Wine Festival (September) or the Lugana Armonie senza Tempo (June) for a festive atmosphere.

Tips for Exploring the Routes:

Best Time to Visit: Spring (April-May): Blooming landscapes and pleasant weather.

Autumn (September-October): Grape and olive harvest season.

Transportation: Rent a car for flexibility, or join guided tours that include transport and tastings.

Stay Safe: If indulging in tastings, consider hiring a driver or opting for group tours.

Reservations: Book tours in advance, especially during weekends and peak tourist seasons.

CHAPTER 5

CULTURAL HIGHLIGHTS

5.1 Local Traditions and Customs of Lake Garda

Lake Garda's cultural tapestry is rich with traditions, customs, and festivals that reflect its deep historical roots and Mediterranean influence. From age-old rituals to vibrant modern celebrations, the local culture offers a glimpse into the lives and values of the communities that call this picturesque region home.

The Olive Harvest. Each autumn, olive groves around Lake Garda buzz with activity as families and workers come together for the olive harvest. It's a time-honored tradition that often involves manual labor to ensure the delicate fruits remain intact.

The Blessing of the Lake (Benedizione del Lago): Annually in early spring. A religious tradition where local priests bless the lake to ensure safe waters and bountiful fish. This event includes a small procession and a festive atmosphere.

Local Craftsmanship: From handcrafted ceramics in Salò to lacework in Desenzano del Garda, traditional crafts are a testament to the region's artistic heritage. Where to Find: Artisan workshops and markets in the towns around the lake.

Customs in Everyday Life

Aperitivo Culture: Much like the rest of Italy, Lake Garda residents embrace the tradition of aperitivo, a pre-dinner ritual involving drinks and light snacks. Locally produced wines like Bardolino or a classic Aperol Spritz are paired with olives, cheese, and cured meats.

Family and Food-Centric Gatherings: Meals are a sacred time for families and often last hours, filled with lively conversation and multiple courses. Sunday lunch, in particular, is an important time for extended families to come together.

Festive Attire and Music: During festivals, you'll see traditional costumes—often a mix of medieval and Renaissance styles, alongside live performances of folk music. Instruments like the accordion and tambourine play a central role.

Festivals and Celebrations

Festa dell'Uva e del Vino (Wine and Grape Festival) Location in Bardolino. Late September to early October. A celebration of the grape harvest with wine tastings, food stalls, music, and fireworks. It's a great way to immerse yourself in local culture.

Notte di Fiaba (Night of Fairy Tales): Location in Riva del. Around August. Its a family-friendly event featuring street performers, fairy tale reenactments, and a grand fireworks display over the lake.

Carnevale di Arco (Arco Carnival): Located in Arco, During February (pre-Lenten season) .Its a lively carnival with parades, masked balls, and elaborate costumes.

Festa di San Giovanni (St. John's Festival): Located in Torbole. During June 24th. Its religious and community celebration with a lakeside bonfire, processions, and traditional food.

Superstitions and Beliefs

The Evil Eye (Malocchio): An old belief in the region involves warding off the evil eye with amulets, hand gestures, or blessings. Good Luck Symbols: Red coral and garlic are believed to bring protection and good fortune.

Water and Prosperity. The lake itself is seen as a symbol of life and prosperity. Locals believe tossing a coin into the lake ensures a return visit or good fortune.

5.2 Art and Music Festivals of Lake Garda

Lake Garda's cultural scene is enriched by a variety of art and music festivals that draw inspiration from its stunning surroundings and historical charm. From classical music echoing through ancient amphitheaters to contemporary art exhibitions in quaint lakeside towns, these events offer something for every art and music enthusiast.

Major Art and Music Festivals

Tener-a-Mente Festival: Locatedin Vittoriale degli Italiani, Gardone Riviera. Around June to August. A celebrated summer festival featuring an eclectic lineup of performances, including classical, jazz, pop, and theatrical acts. The open-air amphitheater provides breathtaking views of the lake, enhancing the experience. Tickets: $40–$100 depending on the performance.

Riva del Garda Music Festival: Located in Riva del Garda. Around Late August. A week-long celebration of classical and contemporary music, featuring orchestras, soloists, and chamber music. Performances take place in historic venues such as churches and piazzas. Free open-air concerts by Lake Garda.

Festa dell'Opera: Located in Verona (a short distance from Lake Garda). Around September. A citywide opera festival that spills into Lake Garda's towns, featuring live performances in squares, courtyards, and even vineyards.Free performances and a mix of classic and modern interpretations of opera.

5.3 Entertainment And Nightlife

Lake Garda offers a vibrant entertainment and nightlife scene, catering to diverse preferences. Here are some notable venues and activities to consider:

ArtClub Disco: Located in Bardolino, ArtClub is renowned for its lively atmosphere and diverse music selection. Entry fees typically range from €10 to €20, depending on the event.

Delirivm Tremens: Situated in Peschiera del Garda, this bar offers a wide selection of craft beers and cocktails. It's a popular spot for both locals and tourists seeking a relaxed evening out. Prices for drinks vary, with beers starting around €5.

Taberna Don Diego: Located in Peschiera del Garda, Taberna Don Diego is a lively bar known for its vibrant atmosphere and live music. It's a popular spot for both locals and tourists seeking a fun night out. Prices for drinks vary, with cocktails starting around €8.

Relax Beach Bardolino: This beach club in Bardolino transforms into a lively venue in the evenings, offering music and drinks by the lake. It's an ideal spot for those looking to enjoy the night with a view. Entry fees and drink prices vary.

Peschiera. The town of Peschiera del Garda boasts a variety of bars and restaurants along its canals, providing a picturesque setting for evening outings. Prices vary depending on the establishment, with drinks typically starting around €5.

Caffe Roma: Located in Sirmione, Caffe Roma is a charming café that offers a relaxed atmosphere, perfect for enjoying a drink in the evening. It's a great spot for couples seeking a romantic setting. Prices for drinks vary, with cocktails starting around €8.

Moby Dick - Lake Garda: Situated in Sirmione, Moby Dick is a popular bar known for its lively atmosphere and music. It's a great spot for groups looking to enjoy a night out. Prices for drinks vary, with beers starting around €5.

Pasticceria Eoliana: Located in Sirmione, Pasticceria Eoliana is a pastry shop that offers a variety of desserts and pastries. It's a great spot for couples looking to enjoy a sweet treat in a romantic setting. Prices for pastries vary, with items starting around €2.

Asso Bar: Situated in Peschiera del Garda, Asso Bar is a popular spot for both locals and tourists seeking a fun night out. Prices for drinks vary, with cocktails starting around €8.

Bar Castello: Located in Malcesine, Bar Castello offers a relaxed atmosphere with stunning views of the lake. It's a great spot for couples looking to enjoy a drink in a romantic setting. Prices for drinks vary, with beers starting around €5.

5.4 Historical Museums and Galleries of Lake Garda

Lake Garda is steeped in history, with its museums and galleries offering captivating insights into the region's past. From ancient Roman relics to medieval artifacts and contemporary art, these institutions provide an enriching cultural experience.

Historical Museums

MAG Museo Alto Garda: Located within the medieval Rocca Fortress, the MAG Museo Alto Garda highlights the region's history, art, and archaeology. Exhibits range from Roman-era artifacts to contemporary art, with a focus on the cultural evolution of the Garda area.

- **Opening Hours:**

    April–October: 10 AM – 6 PM

    November–March: 10 AM – 5 PM (closed Mondays)

- **Entrance Fee**: $7 per adult

Limonaia del Castel: This historic lemon grove offers an immersive experience into the region's citrus-growing traditions. Visitors can explore terraces of lemon trees and learn about ancient farming techniques.

- **Opening Hours:**

    Daily: 10 AM – 7 PM

- **Entrance Fee**: $3 per adult

Museo della Pesca (Fishing Museum): Located in Peschiera del Garda. This small but fascinating museum focuses on the traditional fishing methods of Lake Garda. It's a great spot to learn about the lake's ecological history and the livelihoods of local communities

- **Opening Hours:**

Tuesday–Sunday: 10 AM – 6 PM

- **Entrance Fee**: $5 per adult

Museo Napoleonico (Napoleonic Museum) A museum dedicated to the Napoleonic wars, particularly the battles fought near Lake Garda.

- **Opening Hours**:

    Tuesday–Sunday: 9 AM – 5 PM

- **Entrance Fee**: $6 per adult

Art Galleries

Galleria Civica G.B. Bosio: Located in Desenzano del Garda. This gallery showcases works by local and national artists, with an emphasis on modern and contemporary art.

- **Opening Hours:**

    Wednesday–Sunday: 11 AM – 6 PM

- **Entrance Fee**: $5 per adult

Art Gallery Studio 7: A hub for contemporary art, featuring pieces by emerging and established artists from around Italy.

- **Opening Hours**:

    Thursday–Saturday: 3 PM – 8 PM

- **Entrance Fee**: Free

Villa Romana di Desenzano : This Roman villa houses some of the most well-preserved mosaics in Northern Italy, alongside a small gallery of Roman-era artifacts.

- **Opening Hours:**

    Tuesday–Sunday: 9 AM – 6 PM

- **Entrance Fee**: $4 per adult

5.5 Shopping

Lake Garda isn't just a haven for nature and adventure; it also offers a diverse shopping experience. From quaint local markets to high-end boutiques, and from artisanal products to designer brands, the shopping opportunities around the lake cater to every taste and budget. Whether you're hunting for souvenirs, gourmet foods, or luxury items, the towns and villages around Lake Garda won't disappoint.

Local Markets

Riva del Garda Market, Located in Piazza 3 Novembre, Riva del Garda.
- What to Find: Fresh produce, local cheeses, olive oils, and handmade crafts.
- Opening Time: Every Wednesday morning.
- Prices: Starting at $5 for small souvenirs and $10 for local olive oils.

Desenzano del Garda Market, Located in Town Center, Desenzano del Garda.
- What to Find: A mix of clothing, accessories, and local food specialties.
- Opening Time: Every Tuesday morning.
- Prices: Fresh produce starts at $3 per kilogram; handcrafted items from $15.

Lazise Market, Located in Lazise Waterfront.
- What to Find: Artisanal leather goods, jewelry, and gourmet items like wine and truffle oil.
- Opening Time: Every Wednesday morning.
- Prices: Leather goods from $20; gourmet items from $10.

Shopping Streets and Boutiques

***Via Mazzini**, Verona:* For a touch of high-end luxury, head to Via Mazzini, one of the most famous shopping streets in nearby Verona. You'll find global brands like Gucci, Prada, and Louis Vuitton alongside Italian designers.

- Location: 30 minutes from Lake Garda by car or train.
- Prices: Designer items start at $100.

Peschiera del Garda Old Town: Explore the cobbled streets of Peschiera for boutique shops offering artisanal ceramics, handmade jewelry, and unique clothing.

- Location: Peschiera del Garda, Southern Shore.
- Prices: Jewelry starts at $30; ceramics from $25.

Sirmione: Sirmione's charming streets are filled with artisan shops selling high-quality olive oils, local wines, handmade soaps, and more.

- Location: Sirmione Old Town.
- Prices: Handmade soaps from $10; olive oils from $15.

Malls and Shopping Centers

La Grande Mela Shoppingland
- What to Find: Over 120 stores featuring Italian and international brands, a food court, and a cinema.
- Location: Via Trentino, 1, Bussolengo, about 20 minutes from Lake Garda.
- Prices: Clothing starts at $20; electronics from $50.

Adigeo Shopping Center
- What to Find: A modern shopping mall in Verona with brands like H&M, Zara, and Sephora, plus several dining options.
- Location: Viale delle Nazioni, Verona.
- Prices: Fashion items from $10; cosmetics from $15.

Specialty Shops

OlioCRU (Riva del Garda)
- What to Find: Premium olive oils, balsamic vinegars, and gourmet food products.
- Prices: Olive oils from $20 per bottle.
- Location: Via del Benaco, Riva del Garda.

Garda Wineshop (Bardolino)
- What to Find: A curated selection of local wines, including Bardolino and Lugana, as well as wine accessories.
- Prices: Wine bottles start at $10.
- Location: Bardolino Town Center.

Limone Souvenir Shop (Limone sul Garda)
- What to Find: Lemon-themed items, from soaps to liqueurs and textiles.
- Prices: Lemon soaps from $5; limoncello from $12.
- Location: Limone sul Garda Town Center.

Tips for Shopping Around Lake Garda

- Timing: Markets are typically open in the mornings and close by early afternoon. Shops in tourist towns may stay open until late during the summer months.
- Payment: Credit cards are widely accepted, but smaller markets and stalls may only take cash.
- Shipping: Many high-end boutiques and specialty stores offer shipping services for larger items.
- Bargaining: While it's not common in stores, haggling is sometimes acceptable at markets.

Lake Garda's shopping options provide a delightful mix of tradition and modernity. Whether you're looking for handcrafted souvenirs, gourmet food, or luxury fashion, the area offers something for everyone. Don't forget to leave extra space in your suitcase, you'll want to bring home a piece of Lake Garda!

CHAPTER 6

ACCOMMODATION OPTION

6.1 Boutique Hotels and Luxury Resorts

Lake Garda offers a variety of boutique hotels and luxury resorts, each providing unique experiences for travelers. Here are some notable options:

Boutique Hotel Villa Sostaga Gargnano, Italy A 4-star hotel situated above Lake Garda, offering panoramic views, elegant rooms, and personalized service. Prices start from approximately $140 per person per night.

Hotel Bella Riva Gardone Riviera, Italy A luxury hotel located directly on the lakefront, featuring modern amenities, an outdoor pool, and fine dining. Rates begin at around $200 per person per night.

54

Lefay Resort & SPA Lago di Garda Gargnano, Located at the lower lake side. Italy A 5-star resort focusing on wellness, with extensive spa facilities, sustainable practices, and stunning lake views. Prices start from approximately $300 per person per night.

Cape of Senses Torri del Benaco, Italy A newly opened spa hotel designed for serene wellness retreats, offering expansive views of the lake and surrounding mountains. Rates begin at around $350 per person per night.

Hotel Lido Palace Riva del Garda, Italy A 5-star hotel combining historical architecture with modern design, featuring a luxury spa and gourmet dining. Prices start from approximately $250 per person per night.

6.2 Budget friendly Guesthouse

Lake Garda offers a variety of budget-friendly guesthouses that provide comfortable accommodations without straining your finances. Here are some options to consider:

La Lanterna
Location : Via Torrente Gusa, Garda Veneto
A 3-star guesthouse offering basic amenities and a convenient location near the town center. Prices start at approximately $52 per person per night.

Palme
Location: Garage Vento
An affordable hotel with comfortable rooms, an outdoor pool, and complimentary Wi-Fi. Rates begin at around $113 per person per night.

Hotel Miró
Location: Via Antiche Mura, Garda Veneto
A centrally located hotel offering modern amenities and a complimentary breakfast. Rates begin at around $80 per person per night.

Alessandra
Location: Via Monte Baldo, Garda Veneto
A charming hotel featuring an outdoor pool, garden area, and free breakfast. Prices start at approximately $90 per person per night.

6.3 Camping Site for Outdoor Enthusiast

Lake Garda offers a variety of camping sites that cater to outdoor enthusiasts seeking budget-friendly accommodations. Here are some options to consider:

Camping Eden Gargnano, Italy Located in Gargnano, Camping Eden offers pitches for tents and caravans, as well as mobile homes. Prices for a standard pitch start at €9 per person per night during the low season (April 24 – May 3). Rates increase during peak season, with prices reaching €15 per person per night from June 7 to June 21.

Camping La Quercia Lazise, Italy Situated in Lazise, Camping La Quercia provides a range of camping options, including pitches and mobile homes. Opens from March 27 to October 5. Prices are € 10 - € 13 per person , the campsite offers online reservations and the option to request a free quote for your holiday.

Camping Paradiso Gargnano, Italy Located in Gargnano, Camping Paradiso offers pitches for tents and caravans. Daily prices from April 1 to September 30, 2024, are €10.50 for adults, €8.50 for children (ages 3 to 7), and €3.50 for dogs. Electricity is available for €6.00.

Camping Cisano San Vito Lazise, Italy Situated in Lazise, Camping Cisano San Vito offers pitches for tents and caravans, as well as mobile homes. Opens March to October, prices €25 per person during low season which increases during peak season.

Camping Amici di Lazise Lazise, Italy Located in Lazise, Camping Amici di Lazise provides pitches for tents and caravans, as well as mobile homes. Opens from January 1, 2025 till January 7,2025 February 2, 2025 till December 31, 2025 Price €41 - € 51 per night and vary depending on the accommodation type and season.

CHAPTER 7

WHAT TO EAT AND DRINK

7.1 Traditional Dishes of Lake Garda

Lake Garda's culinary scene is rich with traditional dishes that reflect the region's history and natural resources. Here are some notable dishes to try, along with their typical prices and locations:

Bigoli con le Sarde : A traditional Venetian pasta dish featuring thick, long noodles served with a sauce made from fresh sardines, garlic, and olive oil. This dish is commonly found in restaurants around Lake Garda. Prices typically range from €10 to €15.

Risotto al Pesce Persico: A creamy risotto prepared with perch, a fish native to Lake Garda. The delicate flavor of the perch complements the rich risotto. This dish is popular in the towns surrounding the lake. Prices usually range from €12 to €20.

Tortellini di Valeggio: Delicate pasta parcels filled with a mixture of meat and herbs, originating from the town of Valeggio sul Mincio near Lake Garda. Often served with butter and sage. Prices typically range from €15 to €25.

Luccio in Salsa con Polenta: Pike fish cooked in a savory sauce, accompanied by polenta. Average price: €15-€20. Found in traditional eateries throughout the Lake Garda region.

Polenta e Osei: Polenta served with small game birds, a rustic dish from the area. Average price: €18-€25. Available in select traditional restaurants.

7.2 Local wines: Bardolino and Laguna

Lake Garda is renowned for its exceptional wines, notably Bardolino and Lugana, each offering unique flavors that reflect the region's rich viticultural heritage.

Bardolino Wine: Bardolino is a red wine produced in the Veneto region, particularly around Lake Garda. It's crafted primarily from Corvina, Rondinella, and Molinara grapes, resulting in a light, fresh wine with notes of cherry and plum.

Bardolino Classico DOC by Roccolo del Lago: This wine is available for approximately $12.99 per 750ml bottle.

Bardolino Classico DOC by Zonin: Priced at €8.80 per bottle.

Lugana Wine: Lugana is a white wine produced in the Lombardy region, near the southern shores of Lake Garda. Made predominantly from Turbiana grapes, it offers a crisp, mineral profile with hints of citrus and almond.

Lugana "PRESTIGE" DOC by Cà Maiol: Available for €12.80 per bottle.
Ottella Lugana: This wine averages around $16 per 750ml bottle.

Purchasing Locations

These wines can be found at various retailers and restaurants around lake garda and also online and in physical stores. For instance, Uritalianwines located on the east of lake garda offers a selection of Bardolino wines, including the Bardolino Classico DOC by Zonin.

7.3 Olive Oils

Lake Garda's culinary landscape is enriched by its exceptional olive oils and regional delicacies, each offering a taste of the area's rich heritage. Here are some notable options:

Garda DOP Extra Virgin Olive Oil: This premium olive oil is produced in the Garda Trentino region, known for its delicate flavor and balanced aromas. It features a green to yellow color with a medium fruity scent and a sweet almond aftertaste. Available for approximately €28.65 for a 500ml bottle.

Agraria Riva del Garda Uliva PDO Garda Trentino Olive Oil:
This extra virgin olive oil is crafted from olives grown in the Garda Trentino area, offering a medium fruity profile. Priced at €28.65 for a 500ml bottle.

Agraria Riva del Garda Imperiale PDO Garda Trentino Olive Oil: A premium extra virgin olive oil with a medium fruity taste, reflecting the unique terroir of the Garda Trentino region. Available for €23.77 for a 500ml bottle.

Agraria Riva del Garda Uliva 1111 Olive Oil: This high-quality extra virgin olive oil offers a medium fruity flavor, ideal for enhancing various dishes. Priced at €71.02 for a 250ml bottle.

Agraria Riva del Garda Bonamini Extra Virgin Olive Oil
A light fruity extra virgin olive oil, perfect for those who prefer a milder taste. Available for €22.98 for a 500ml bottle.
These olive oils can be purchased directly from the producers' or through specialized retailers around the lake.

7.4 Best Restaurants and Hidden Gems

Lake Garda boasts a diverse culinary scene, featuring both renowned restaurants and hidden gems that offer authentic regional flavors. Here are some notable establishments:

Il Girasole: Located Via Vittorio Emanuele, Sirmione Lombardia
Offers some of the best food on the lake, with a menu that showcases local specialties. Price per meal: $10

Osteria La Miniera: Located Via Chiesa, Tignale Lombardia
A restaurant that combines traditional flavors with a modern twist, set in a unique location. Price per meal: $20

La Locanda del Benaco: Located in Lungo Lago Giuseppe Zanardelli, Salò Lombardia. Known for its refined dishes and elegant setting, offering a memorable dining experience. Price per meal: $17

Osteria dell'Orologio: Located via Butturini 26/a, Salò Lombardia
A charming eatery offering a variety of local dishes in a cozy atmosphere. Price per meal $15

CHAPTER 8

DAY TRIPS AND EXCURSIONS

8.1 Discovering the Dolomite

The Dolomites, a UNESCO World Heritage site, are a stunning mountain range located just a short drive from Lake Garda. This natural wonder offers a dramatic contrast to the tranquil beauty of the lake, making it an ideal day trip for nature lovers, adventurers, and photography enthusiasts.

Exploring the Dolomites: A Guide

Hiking and Nature Walks: The Dolomites are famous for their towering peaks, lush valleys, and picturesque alpine lakes. There are numerous trails catering to various levels of experience, from easy walks to challenging hikes. One of the most popular routes is the Tre Cime di Lavaredo loop, which offers breathtaking views of the iconic three peaks.

- Duration: 5 to 7 hours (for more challenging hikes).
- Price: Free for most trails, though some areas charge a small entrance fee of around €5–€10.
- Location: Dolomiti di Sesto (South Tyrol), approximately 2-2.5 hours from Lake Garda.

Cable Cars and Scenic Rides: For those who prefer a more relaxed way to take in the Dolomites' majesty, the cable cars and funiculars provide easy access to panoramic viewpoints. The Marmolada Glacier, the highest peak in the Dolomites, is accessible via cable car from the village of Malga Ciapela.

- Price: Around €20–€30 for a round trip.
- Location: Marmolada, 2.5 hours from Lake Garda.

Cortina d'Ampezzo: Often referred to as the "Pearl of the Dolomites," Cortina d'Ampezzo is a charming alpine town known for its luxury shopping, high-end restaurants, and stunning mountain views. It's a perfect place to stop for lunch or spend a few hours exploring.

- Price: Free to visit, but expect to pay around €15–€30 for a meal at a restaurant.
- Location: About 2 hours from Lake Garda.

Lago di Braies (Lake Braies): One of the most iconic spots in the Dolomites, Lago di Braies is known for its emerald-green waters and surrounding mountain peaks. A leisurely boat ride on the lake is a must-do, or you can enjoy a peaceful walk around its shoreline.

- Price: €5 for parking, €15 for boat rental (per hour).
- Location: 2.5 hours from Lake Garda.

Driving the Dolomite Road (Great Dolomite Road): This scenic driving route takes you through the heart of the Dolomites, passing through beautiful mountain passes, alpine villages, and offering stunning views at every turn. It's perfect for a road trip if you want to explore the mountains at your own pace.

- Price: Free (except for occasional tolls).
- Location: The route starts from Bolzano and runs through various picturesque towns and mountain areas, about 2.5 to 3 hours from Lake Garda.

How to Get There

By Car: The Dolomites are easily accessible by car from Lake Garda. You can take the A22 motorway from the southern part of the lake, heading toward the Trentino-Alto Adige region. From there, a series of mountain roads will lead you to your desired destination in the Dolomites.

By Train and Bus: For those without a car, there are regular bus and train services that connect Lake Garda with Dolomite towns like

Cortina d'Ampezzo and Bolzano. From these towns, local buses or taxis can take you to popular sights.

When to Visit

Summer: Ideal for hiking, cycling, and outdoor activities with warm weather and clear skies.

Winter: A popular destination for skiing and winter sports.

Whether you're looking to explore the Dolomites on foot, by bike, or through a scenic drive, this natural wonderland offers unforgettable experiences and breathtaking landscapes.

8.2 Verona: The City of Love

Verona, located just 30 minutes from Lake Garda, is one of Italy's most romantic and historically rich cities. Known globally as the setting of Shakespeare's Romeo and Juliet, Verona combines medieval charm with stunning Renaissance architecture, making it a must-visit destination for any trip to the region.

Why Visit Verona?

Romantic Heritage (The Juliet's House): Verona's claim to fame as the *"City of Love"* largely stems from its association with the timeless story of Romeo and Juliet. You can visit Casa di Giulietta (Juliet's House), where you'll find the famous balcony where Juliet is said to have spoken to Romeo. Visitors often leave love notes on the walls or pose for pictures under the iconic balcony.

- Price: €6 entry fee for the house and museum.
- Location: Via Cappello, 23, 37121 Verona.

Piazza delle Erbe (Heart of Verona): Verona's main square, Piazza delle Erbe, is one of the most charming in Italy, surrounded by impressive buildings such as the Torre dei Lamberti, the Mazzanti Houses, and the Palazzo Maffei. It's a great spot to relax with a coffee, wander through the local market, or visit the historical Casa dei Mercanti.

- Price: Free to visit the square; climbing the Torre dei Lamberti costs €8.
- Location: Piazza delle Erbe, 37121 Verona.

Verona Arena: The Arena di Verona is one of the best-preserved Roman amphitheaters in Italy, second only to the Colosseum in Rome. It hosts open-air operas and concerts during the summer, attracting thousands of visitors. Even if you don't attend a performance, the Arena is a magnificent site to explore.

- Price: €10 for entry to the Arena.
- Location: Piazza Bra, 37121 Verona.

Castelvecchio: The Castelvecchio is a medieval fortress housing a museum dedicated to Verona's history, art, and culture. The castle is particularly notable for its impressive architecture, beautiful bridge, and scenic views of the Adige River.

- Price: €10 for the museum.
- Location: Corso Castelvecchio, 37121 Verona.

Piazza dei Signori: This beautiful square is surrounded by impressive buildings, including the Palazzo della Ragione, the Loggia del Consiglio, and the Torre dei Lamberti. The square is home to many cafes, and it's a perfect spot for a leisurely stroll or an evening aperitif.
- Price: Free to visit the square.
- Location: Piazza dei Signori, 37121 Verona.

Other Highlight:

Basilica di San Zeno Maggiore: A stunning Romanesque church with beautiful frescoes and the tomb of Saint Zeno, the patron saint of Verona.

Giardino Giusti: A beautiful Renaissance garden perfect for a relaxing walk with breathtaking views of the city.

Ponte Pietra: An ancient Roman bridge offering fantastic views of Verona's historic center.

How to Get to Verona from Lake Garda

- **By Car**: Verona is easily accessible by car, just a 30-minute drive from the southern shore of Lake Garda.

- **By Train**: From Peschiera del Garda or Desenzano del Garda, you can catch a train to Verona, which takes about 15–20 minutes.

- **By Bus**: There are also regular bus services from Lake Garda to Verona.

When to Visit Verona

Spring and Summer: Ideal for exploring the city's outdoor attractions and enjoying the open-air performances at the Verona Arena.
Autumn and Winter: The city becomes quieter and more intimate, with fewer tourists, making it perfect for a peaceful visit and romantic walks.

Best Time for Romance in Verona

Verona is not just the City of Love because of its Shakespearean connection but also due to its atmosphere. Whether you're walking through the narrow, cobbled streets or sitting in a café in Piazza delle Erbe, Verona exudes romance year-round. For an extra romantic experience, visit in the evening when the city is lit up and enjoy dinner in one of its charming restaurants.

8.3 Venice: A Romantic Getaway

Known as one of the most romantic cities in the world, Venice offers an enchanting escape, where every narrow canal, historic building, and charming alleyway tells a story of love, art, and history. Located about 2 hours from Lake Garda, Venice is the perfect destination for couples seeking a magical retreat, art lovers, and those intrigued by its rich history and distinctive charm.

Why Visit Venice?

The Grand Canal: Venice's Lifeblood: The Grand Canal is the heart of Venice, lined with magnificent buildings that showcase the city's rich architectural history. Whether you're taking a romantic gondola ride or a vaporetto (water bus), cruising down this iconic waterway is one of the best ways to soak in the sights of Venice.

Vaporetto (Water Bus): €7.50 per ride, or a multi-day pass can be purchased starting from €20 for 24 hours.

Piazza San Marco (St. Mark's Square): The world-famous Piazza San Marco is the central square of Venice, home to the iconic St. Mark's Basilica and the Campanile (bell tower). The square is a perfect spot to relax, enjoy a coffee, and people-watch while soaking up the atmosphere of one of the most beautiful public spaces in the world.
- Price: Free to visit the square, but entry to St. Mark's Basilica is €3, and climbing the Campanile costs €8.
- Location: Piazza San Marco, 30124 Venice.

St. Mark's Basilica:(A Masterpiece of Byzantine Art): One of the most significant landmarks in Venice, St. Mark's Basilica is known for its stunning mosaics, golden domes, and intricate architecture. The basilica's opulence and historical significance make it a must-see during any visit to Venice.

- Price: Free entry to the basilica, with a fee for special areas like the museum or the treasury (€5–€10).

- Location: Piazza San Marco, 30124 Venice.

The Rialto Bridge

One of the oldest and most iconic bridges in Venice, the Rialto Bridge spans the Grand Canal. It's the perfect place for a photo opportunity, as the bridge offers stunning views of the canal and the bustling market area beneath.
- Price: Free to visit.
- Location: Rialto, 30125 Venice.

Gondola Ride Through the Canals
No trip to Venice is complete without a gondola ride. These traditional Venetian boats offer a peaceful and intimate way to explore the city's narrow canals, past charming buildings and beneath centuries-old bridges. While gondola rides are on the expensive side, the experience is undeniably romantic.

- Price: Around €80 for a 30-minute ride, with some gondoliers offering longer rides at higher prices.
- Location: Gondola stations are located near Piazza San Marco and Rialto Bridge.

8.4 Gardaland and Caneva Aquapark: Family Fun and Adventure on Lake Garda

For families, thrill-seekers, and anyone looking to add a bit of excitement to their Lake Garda experience, Gardaland and Caneva Aquapark offer two of the most popular attractions in the region. These amusement parks are perfect for all ages, featuring rides, shows, water attractions, and a day filled with fun.

Gardaland : Is one of the largest and most famous amusement parks in Italy, attracting millions of visitors each year. Located near the town of Castelnuovo del Garda, it is a must-visit destination for anyone visiting Lake Garda, especially families and thrill-seekers.

Thrilling Rides: Gardaland is home to a wide range of thrilling roller coasters, such as the Shaman, a ride that blends physical sensations with a captivating story of ancient rituals and nature, and Blue Tornado, an inverted coaster that spins riders through dizzying loops. For those looking for a bit less adrenaline, attractions like the Pirate Ship and Jungle Rapids offer a fun experience for all ages.

For Younger Visitors: Gardaland also caters to younger visitors with gentler rides and experiences like Fantasy Kingdom, where children can meet their favorite characters and ride on friendly attractions such as The Carousel and Magic Mountain.

Themed Zones: The park is divided into several themed areas, such as Medieval Kingdom, Far West, and Adventure Land, each offering immersive experiences and rides related to its theme. These zones help enhance the atmosphere and make the day feel like a journey through different worlds.

Shows and Entertainment: Throughout the day, Gardaland also offers a variety of live shows, from stunt performances to musical theater. These performances add an extra layer of excitement and entertainment for guests.

- Opening hours: Gardaland is typically open from April to October, with varying hours depending on the season (usually from 10:00 AM to 6:00 PM).

- Ticket Prices: A full-day adult ticket typically costs around €40–€45, with discounts for children, groups, and multi-day tickets. There are also special packages that include skip-the-line tickets and access to special experiences.
- Location: Via Derna, 4, 37014 Castelnuovo del Garda VR, Italy.

Caneva Aquapark: Just a short drive from Gardaland, Caneva Aquapark is a water park that offers an ideal escape during the hot summer months. Located in Lazise, this exciting water park features attractions for all ages, from gentle pools to thrilling water slides.

Water Slides and Attractions: Caneva Aquapark is home to a variety of water slides, including adrenaline-pumping slides like Kamikaze (a steep slide for the daring) and Black Hole, where visitors slide into total darkness. For those who prefer a slower pace, there are the Lazy River, a relaxing float along the water, and the Wave Pool, which creates waves that mimic the ocean's rhythm.

Kid-Friendly Areas : Younger children will love the Children's Area, which is equipped with small slides, water jets, and themed attractions. There are also areas designed for toddlers, making it a perfect place for families with kids of all ages.

Themed Zones: The park is divided into various themed zones like Tropical Lagoon, with its lush landscaping and water features, and Rio Bravo, which has Western-themed slides.

Relaxation Areas: For those who want to take it easy, there are plenty of shaded areas, loungers, and spaces to relax by the pool or near the water.

- Caneva Aquapark is typically open from May to September, with extended hours in peak summer months (usually 10:00 AM to 6:00 PM or later).
- Ticket Prices: Adult tickets cost around €25–€30, while children's tickets range from €20–€25 depending on height. Group tickets and family packages are available at discounted rates.
- Location: Località Lazise VR, Italy.

Combining Gardaland and Caneva Aquapark: A Day of Thrills and Water Fun

For those who want to experience both the thrills of Gardaland and the refreshing fun of Caneva Aquapark, a combined ticket can be purchased, allowing you to visit both parks in a single day. This is a great option for those who want a full day of adventure without the hassle of purchasing separate tickets for each park.

- Combined Ticket Price: Typically, a combined ticket for both Gardaland and Caneva Aquapark costs around €60–€70 per adult, depending on the time of year and available promotions.

How to Get There

By Car: Both Gardaland and Caneva Aquapark are located in the same area, near Lazise and Castelnuovo del Garda, making it easy to access both by car. Parking is available at each park for a fee (around €6–€10 per day).

By Train: The nearest train stations are Peschiera del Garda and Verona, both of which are well-connected to the amusement parks by bus or taxi.

8.5 Boat Tour And Cruise Lake Garda

Lake Garda offers a variety of boat tours and cruises, each providing unique perspectives of the lake's stunning landscapes and charming towns. Here are some notable options to consider:

Lake Garda Mini Cruise: Sirmione Peninsula
This 25-minute mini cruise explores the Sirmione Peninsula, offering views of historical sites and natural beauty. Prices start at approximately $13 per person. Departures are from Sirmione.

Castles Boat Tour with Bardolino Wine Tasting
This tour combines sightseeing with wine tasting, featuring visits to lakeside castles and sampling of local Bardolino wine. Prices start at

around $104 per person. Departures are available from various locations around the lake.

Sunset Tour in Sirmione
Experience the beauty of Lake Garda at sunset on this tour departing from Sirmione. Prices start at approximately $13 per person.

Private Romantic Motorboat Tour from Sirmione
Ideal for couples seeking a personalized experience, this private motorboat tour departs from Sirmione. Prices and availability vary; please check with the provider for details.

Lake Garda: Historic Castle Cruise with Wine Tasting
This cruise offers views of historic castles along Lake Garda,

complemented by wine tasting. Prices and departure locations vary; please consult the provider for specifics.

CHAPTER 9

ITINERARY

9.1 5-Day Itinerary for Lake Garda: Exploring the Best of the Lake

This 5-day itinerary is designed to help you experience the highlights of Lake Garda, balancing adventure, culture, relaxation, and gastronomy. Each day focuses on a different region of the lake, offering a well-rounded exploration.

Day 1: Southern Shore – Sirmione and Desenzano del Garda
Highlights: History, relaxation, and picturesque views.

> *Morning*: Begin your day in Sirmione, known as the "Pearl of Lake Garda."
> Visit Scaliger Castle (entry: $10) and explore its history.
> Take a walk to the Grotte di Catullo, an ancient Roman villa with stunning lake views (entry: $7).
>
> **Lunch**: Enjoy local specialties like bigoli pasta at Ristorante Al Boccone, Sirmione (average meal: $25).
>
> *Afternoon:* Drive or take a ferry to Desenzano del Garda.
> Visit the Roman Villa for its mosaics and historical significance (entry: $6). Stroll along the harbor and enjoy gelato at Gelateria Venturelli.
>
> *Evening*: Relax with a lakeside dinner at Trattoria Alessi (average meal: $30).

Day 2: Western Shore – Limone sul Garda and Salò
Highlights: Lemon groves, peaceful retreats, and charming promenades.

Morning: Head to Limone sul Garda, famous for its lemon groves.

Visit the Limonaia del Castel, an open-air lemon museum (entry: $4).

Walk along the scenic Ciclopista del Garda, one of the most beautiful cycling routes in the world.

Lunch: Have a lakeside meal at Ristorante Monte Baldo in Limone (average meal: $25)

Afternoon: Drive or ferry to Salò, known for its historic charm and promenade.

Visit the MuSa Museum to learn about local history and art (entry: $8).

Evening: Dine at Ristorante Da Vittorio in Salò, renowned for its fresh fish dishes (average meal: $35).

Day 3: Northern Shore – Riva del Garda and Torbole
Highlights: Outdoor adventures and breathtaking scenery.

Morning: Begin in Riva del Garda with a hike to Bastione, a medieval fort offering panoramic views of the lake.

Visit the MAG Museum to explore the area's cultural heritage (entry: $5).

Lunch: Enjoy a meal at Ristorante Pizzeria Leon d'Oro in Riva (average meal: $20).

Afternoon: Head to Torbole, a windsurfing paradise.

Rent equipment or take a windsurfing lesson (from $60/hour) or enjoy a relaxing walk along the promenade.

Evening: Return to Riva for a cozy dinner at Osteria La Contrada (average meal: $30).

Day 4: Eastern Shore – Malcesine and Bardolino

Highlights: Castles, wine, and scenic beauty.

> **Morning**: Explore Malcesine, starting with a visit to Scaliger Castle (entry: $6).
> Take the Monte Baldo Cable Car for breathtaking views of the lake and surrounding mountains (round trip: $25).
> **Lunch:** Enjoy a meal at Al Gondoliere in Malcesine (average meal: $30).
> **Afternoon:** Drive to Bardolino, famous for its wines.
> Visit the Museo del Vino and enjoy wine tasting at a local vineyard (entry and tasting: $15-$20).
> Evening:
> Dine at Taverna Kus in Bardolino, offering traditional dishes and local wine pairings (average meal: $35).

Day 5: Day Trip – Verona or Dolomites

Option 1: Verona – The City of Love

> **Morning:** Drive or take a train to Verona (30 minutes from Lake Garda).
> Visit Juliet's Balcony and Piazza delle Erbe.
> Explore Verona Arena, an ancient Roman amphitheater (entry: $12).
> **Lunch:** Dine at Antica Bottega del Vino, a historic wine bar (average meal: $40).
> **Afternoon:** Stroll through Castelvecchio Museum and along the Adige River.
> **Evening:** Return to Lake Garda.

Option 2: The Dolomites – Alpine Escape

> **Morning**: Take a guided tour or drive to the Dolomites (2 hours from Lake Garda).
> Visit Lago di Braies or take a scenic hike in Val di Funes.
> **Lunch:**

Enjoy hearty alpine cuisine at a mountain hut (rifugio), with dishes like polenta and local cheese (average meal: $25).

Afternoon: Continue exploring the Dolomites' breathtaking landscapes.
Evening: Return to Lake Garda for your final night.

Tips for a Successful Trip

Transportation: Use a mix of ferries, cars, and bikes to explore efficiently.

Reservations: Book accommodations, restaurants, and activities in advance, especially during peak seasons.

Packing: Bring comfortable shoes for walking and hiking, along with layers for varying weather conditions.

This 5-day itinerary ensures a memorable trip, showcasing Lake Garda's stunning natural beauty, rich history, and vibrant culture.

CHAPTER 10

PRACTICAL TIPS FOR TRAVELLERS

10.1 Essential travel documents

When planning your trip to Lake Garda, Italy, it's essential to ensure you have the necessary travel documents to facilitate a smooth journey. Here's an updated guide to help you prepare:

Passport Requirements

- Validity: Your passport must be valid for at least three months beyond your intended departure date from Italy.

- Blank Pages: Ensure your passport has sufficient blank pages for entry and exit stamps.

ETIAS Travel Authorization

Starting in mid-2025, travelers from visa-exempt countries, including the United States, Canada, and the United Kingdom, will need to obtain an ETIAS (European Travel Information and Authorization System) authorization to enter Italy and other Schengen Area countries.

- Application: The ETIAS application is completed online and requires a valid passport, an email address, and a credit or debit card for the €7 fee.

- Validity: Once approved, ETIAS is valid for three years or until your passport expires, whichever comes first.

Processing Time: Most applications are processed within minutes, but it's advisable to apply at least 96 hours before your departure.

Health Insurance

Coverage: While not mandatory, it's highly recommended to have travel health insurance that covers medical expenses, accidents, and repatriation during your stay in Italy.

EHIC/GHIC: EU citizens should carry their European Health Insurance Card (EHIC) or Global Health Insurance Card (GHIC) to access public healthcare services in Italy.

COVID-19 Considerations

Current Status: As of January 2025, Italy has lifted all COVID-19-related entry requirements.

Precautions: It's advisable to carry digital or printed copies of your vaccination certificate or recent test results, as some establishments may still require proof of vaccination or a negative test result.

Additional Tips

- Driver's License: If you plan to rent a car, bring your valid driver's license. Non-EU citizens may also need an International Driving Permit.

- Emergency Contacts: Keep a list of emergency contacts, including your country's embassy or consulate in Italy.

- Local Laws and Customs: Familiarize yourself with local laws and customs to ensure a respectful and lawful visit.

By ensuring all your travel documents are in order, you'll be well-prepared to enjoy the beauty and culture of Lake Garda without any administrative concerns.

10.2 Language basics and local phrases

When traveling to Lake Garda, Italy, familiarizing yourself with basic Italian phrases can greatly enhance your experience. Here are some essential expressions to help you navigate daily interactions:

Greetings and Polite Expressions

Hello/Goodbye: Ciao! (informal)

Good morning: Buongiorno!

Good evening: Buonasera!

Good night: Buonanotte!

Please: Per favore

Thank you: Grazie

You're welcome: Prego

Excuse me: Mi scusi (formal) / Scusa (informal)

I'm sorry: Mi dispiace

Introductions

My name is...: Mi chiamo...

What's your name?: Come si chiama? (formal) / Come ti chiami? (informal)

Nice to meet you: Piacere di conoscerti

Essential Questions

Do you speak English?: Parla inglese?

I don't understand: Non capisco

Can you help me?: Mi può aiutare?

Where is the bathroom?: Dov'è il bagno?

How much does it cost?: Quanto costa?

Directions

Where is...?: Dov'è...?

The train station: la stazione ferroviaria

The bus stop: la fermata dell'autobus

The hotel: l'hotel

The restaurant: il ristorante

Dining

A table for two, please: Un tavolo per due, per favore

The menu, please: Il menù, per favore

I would like...: Vorrei...

The check, please: Il conto, per favore

Numbers

One: Uno

Two: Due

Three: Tre

Four: Quattro

Five: Cinque

Ten: Dieci

Days of the Week

Monday: Lunedì

Tuesday: Martedì

Wednesday: Mercoledì

Thursday: Giovedì

Friday: Venerdì

Saturday: Sabato

Sunday: Domenica

Emergency

Help!: Aiuto!

Call the police: Chiami la polizia

I need a doctor: Ho bisogno di un dottore

10.3 Currency for Lake Garda

Planning your finances is crucial for a stress-free trip to Lake Garda. From currency information to budgeting tips, here's an in-depth guide:

Currency in Italy

Currency Used: The official currency in Italy is the Euro (€), abbreviated as EUR.

- Common Denominations:

    Coins: €0.01, €0.02, €0.05, €0.10, €0.20, €0.50, €1, €2

    Banknotes: €5, €10, €20, €50, €100, €200, €500

- Exchange Rates

Exchange rates fluctuate daily. As of today, 1 USD = approximately 0.93 EUR. Check real-time exchange rates before your trip using apps like XE or OANDA.

How to Get Euros

- ATMs: Widely available in towns around Lake Garda. Italian ATMs often have competitive exchange rates and are easy to use.

- Currency Exchange Offices: Found in major towns like Riva del Garda and Desenzano. Rates here may include a service fee.

- Banks: Offer currency exchange but may have limited hours, especially on weekends.

- Credit/Debit Cards: Most establishments accept cards, especially Visa and Mastercard. AmEx and Discover are less commonly accepted.

Tip: Notify your bank of your travel dates to avoid your card being flagged for suspicious activity.

Money-Saving Tips

- Public Transport: Use ferries and buses instead of renting a car.

- Local Markets: Buy fresh produce and snacks at local markets for an affordable meal option.

- Free Attractions: Explore public beaches, walking trails, and town squares.

Off-Peak Travel: Visit during shoulder seasons (spring or autumn) for lower prices on accommodation and activities.

Useful Apps

- XE Currency: For real-time exchange rates.

- Splitwise: To track group expenses.

- Trail Wallet: Helps monitor your daily travel budget.

By planning ahead and budgeting wisely, you'll be able to enjoy all the beauty and charm of Lake Garda without worrying about financial surprises!

10.4 Safety and Health Tips

When planning a trip to Lake Garda, Italy, it's essential to prioritize safety and health to ensure a pleasant experience. Here are some updated tips to help you stay informed and prepared:

Health Precautions

- **Norovirus Outbreak**: In mid-2024, Torri del Benaco, a village on Lake Garda's shores, experienced a significant norovirus outbreak, leading to over 300 hospitalizations.

- **Preventive Measures:** Hand Hygiene: Regularly wash your hands with soap and water, especially before eating.

Food Safety: Ensure that food is thoroughly cooked and sourced from reputable establishments.

Avoid Contaminated Water: Drink bottled or treated water, and avoid swallowing water while swimming.

More safety Tips

Petty Theft: While Lake Garda is generally safe, be cautious of pickpocketing in tourist areas.

Precautions:

- Secure Valuables: Use money belts or anti-theft bags.

- Stay Vigilant: Be aware of your surroundings, especially in crowded places.

- Avoid Unattended Belongings: Do not leave personal items unattended in public areas.

Traffic Regulations:

- Speed Limits: Adhere to local speed limits to avoid fines.

- Parking: Use designated parking areas to prevent penalties.

- Bicyclists and Motorcyclists: Be cautious of cyclists and motorcyclists, especially on winding roads.

Local Regulations:

- Dress Code: In certain towns around Lake Garda, there are regulations prohibiting men from going shirtless and women from wearing only swimwear in public areas.

- Fines: Violations can result in fines up to $700.

Emergency Contacts

- Emergency Number: Dial 112 for police, medical, or fire emergencies.

Local Healthcare:

EHIC/GHIC: EU citizens should carry their European Health Insurance Card (EHIC) or Global Health Insurance Card (GHIC) to access public healthcare services.

Travel Insurance: Non-EU travelers should have comprehensive travel insurance covering medical emergencies.

Environmental Considerations

- **Sun Protection:**
  Sunscreen: Use broad-spectrum sunscreen to protect against UV radiation.

Hydration: Carry a reusable water bottle to stay hydrated; tap water is generally safe to drink.

- **Swimming Safety:**
  Designated Areas: Swim in marked zones and heed local advisories.
  Supervision: Always supervise children near water bodies.

By staying informed and taking these precautions, you can enjoy a safe and healthy visit to Lake Garda.

SCAN HERE FOR THE CITY'S GENERAL MAP

I know you might probably be wondering if I won't add the general Lake map, well, please worry less, Pamela got you covered, you know your satisfaction is my major concern. Please kindly scan the below QR code or click link https://tinyurl.com/Lake-Garda-Map to access Lake Garda's general map. Once you scan the barcode, all you have to do next is to input the name of the exact location you are heading to.

Thank you so much for purchasing my book in the first place, and thanks a million for reading it.

Tell your own Adventure Story Today

My name:

- _____

I travelled along with:

- _____

I arrival experience:

- _____

- _____

- _____

Where to visit:

- _____

- _____

- _____

Where to Eat:

- _____

- _____

- _____

Transit to use:
- _____
- _____
- _____

Where to stay: check-in time and date:

- _____
- _____
- _____
- _____
- _____
- _____
- _____
- _____

Outdoor activities to take part in:

- _____
- _____
- _____

- _____

- _____

- _____

- _____

Personal Drafted Day trips itinerary:

Day 1:
- _____

- _____

- _____

Day 2:
- _____

- _____

- _____

Day 3:
- _____

- _____

- _____

Share your Lake Garda travel experience:

-
-
-
-
-
-
-
-
-
-
-
-

Printed in Dunstable, United Kingdom